ROUGH

Rough

A collection of poems
by

R. NIKOLAS MACIOCI

BOOKS

Adelaide Books
New York / Lisbon
2020

ROUGH
A collection of poems
By R. Nikolas Macioci

Published by Adelaide Books, New York / Lisbon
adelaidebooks.org

Editor-in-Chief
Stevan V. Nikolic

For any information, please address Adelaide Books
at info@adelaidebooks.org
or write to:
Adelaide Books
244 Fifth Ave. Suite D27
New York, NY, 10001

ISBN: 978-1-953510-66-2

Printed in the United States of America

With much love and thankfulness for my wonderous best friend, Sandra Feen, without whom the journey would have been even rougher.

Contents

Acknowledgment

"Heroin: An Interview" *Black Fox Literary Magazine*

"Saying Grace With the Freaks" *Chiron*

"A Thousand Alienations" *The RavensPerch*

"Going Back" *The RavensPerch*

"Rain and Retribution" *Coal Hill Review*

To

Love

An Addict

Is To

Run Out Of Tears

—*Sandy Swenson*

The Beginniing Well Remembered

Thoughts of you hurt like arrows in the throat.
All day I've fought words in my brain
that drag scenes back into consciousness.

You approached me with a thumbs up
and well-planned scam to sabotage my heart.
That's how it can happen in a saloon, and it
did four and a half years ago. I sat at a slot
machine in the corner, hit three red sevens,
and turned toward the bar. You left your seat
and came to stand beside me as if to encourage
my next win. You had a Madonna-like face
and green eyes that could spot an easy mark.
In a weak and generous moment I handed you
my winnings, and we slept together that night.
I knew that wasn't the way to love somebody,
but I didn't know yet that you were a user
in all senses of the word.

I gave constant pocket money, learned later
you bought heroin. You played me
for desperate, and that is when I realized
you had become my addiction.

After much effort I'm glad to be south of you,
but today is one of those weaker afternoons I keep
slapping my mind with memory.

Tonight I will write about this, waiting for better
judgment to restore equilibrium, or in other words
to be rid of you again.

Blossoms

I walked alone along South High Street
admiring a row of four mock cherry trees
dressed in alabaster. You did not walk
with me but stayed in the car while I
snapped pictures of trees bowed down
in white. I missed you even though you
were only feet away. Sunlight glared,
made blossoms gleam, and I snapped
shots that looked as if they'd been
shaped by snowfall. How could I know
then that the death of our relationship
would soon be news to me and wound
an April day. I continued photographing
while blossoms fell at my feet.

I shouldered my camera and returned
to the car. At first you did not speak,
but your winter eyes pressed into me.
Unprepared to hear you admit a drug
addiction, acid rose in my throat. I did
not speak for a few moments. You said
you hadn't told me before because you
knew I wouldn't understand, and I didn't.

I drove around the neighborhood with
burning in my chest. I remained silent,
angry when I dropped you off. You said
you were sorry and walked inside.

I knew then that it would always come
down either to me or drugs, and I couldn't
compete with heroin.

As I drove away I noticed a few blossoms
had caught under the windshield wipers,
edges already rusty with the beginning
of their end.

Requiem for Groceries

Hungry, without money, groceries, you turn
to me. I drive you to buy whatever you want
or need. Snow, rain, ice doesn't kept us from
trekking to Kroger.

Like a kid, you practically gallop ahead down
aisles, always ahead. It intrigues and annoys
me how you violently throw items into the cart
as if you are mad at them. I study you from
behind. Gray sweats hang loose on your
emaciated frame, still you maintain a dancer's
body. For the moment I have persuaded you
away from smoking by obtaining e-cigarettes;
nevertheless, you always ask me to purchase
several packs which I assume you sell for drugs.

I pay, and you load sacks into the trunk.
The bill often amounts to more than a hundred
dollars. Sometimes I relinquish every cent I have.
I suspect that many of the items are consumed
by other people in the house where you live,
all of whom are drug addicts, an environment
I wish I could extract you from.

You always thank me, but I never know for sure
that you appreciate my sacrifice,
how I consistently empty my pockets for you.

Wednesday Morning

I will spend the rest of my lifetime in
meditation, angry and barren, waiting
for your amends. I am reluctant to change
my prayers to override the love I had for you.
I open the garage door and watch gray drizzle
on the driveway. I was slow as yeast rising
to recognize your scam. I don't smoke
or drink coffee or have any habit to rest
weariness on. I simply stare at rain, recognize
I was an easy mark. I let you into my life,
once free from caregiving for family.
You spotted me in a bar, stood next to me,
your plot to seduce my ready-made loneliness.
In time your constant leaning
against the car window, falling asleep in
my presence, slowly sketched into my
awareness your addiction to pills and drugs.

The rain lures me into wanting to let go
of everything that troubled the last four
years with you, but forgiveness is sidetracked,
and I am drenched in obsessive thoughts about
your infidelity, the impregnation of someone
secretly hidden from me.

R. Nikolas Macioci

Rain begins to gush from the downspouts.
I close the garage door and enter the house,
determined to rid myself of the jagged image
of you that, like glass, still slices my heart.

Easy Rapture

I can't forgive you for showing me silver needles
that silken you into easy rapture, leave me
wishing I hadn't seen your arms full of holes.
You walk out to the dealer waiting in the alley
to be paid with pocket money I have given you.
At that moment I want to turn away from truth
that I have become an enabler.

Back in the house you droop onto the bed,
and I read you a poem about feeling
someone else's pain. I want to be drunk myself,
share oblivion. I have lost patience with your selfish
escape, sticking needles into yourself for instant
bliss while I hassle with whatever the world throws
at me. I envy you subduing agony of living
with drugs, angry with your moral dishonesty.

You are a sad, young man with no job
and no money, living off other people
who are swept away by your youth and bad-boy
appeal. In the complex networking
of the South End you move from person to person,
place to place, handout to handout.

I'm going home now and will write about
what pulses through your veins.

Poetry in the Veins

You think of heroin as poetry
in the veins. At some point you have prowled
everywhere in the South End for a fix,
at times settled for a bag of marijuana.
When you can afford it, you prefer the poke
of a needle two or three times a day.

Even though cops have been honing in on the
neighborhood, under a hoodie and passing
as a teenager, you forage alleys and side streets
to connect with dealers who offer you dangerous
credit. I can't count times you've left me sitting
in the car in a high-risk area for an interminable
time while you scouted out narcotics.

Naive and vulnerable, I had never been
exposed to your way of life before, so
I drove you to shadowy houses,
oblivious of the peril, of what I was
jeopardizing.

One night you left me waiting
in the car forty-five minutes when you
entered a ramshackled house. I became

angry at your inconsideration, slammed
the car door shut, and entered the house.
It was dark inside, but I climbed rickety
stairs to the second floor, threw open the
bedroom door, and found you leaning against
the wall among five other people smoking
marijuana. I flew down the stairs. You
followed, yelled my name, shouted for me
to wait.

And I did wait for four regrettable
years with nothing to remember but deceit,
deception, infidelity, and nights you exposed
me to the possibility of arrest.

Heroin: An Interview

Where do you put the needles, I ask. Arms,
legs, stomach, hands, you answer. What
does it feel like, I ask. You get to edge
your way off the earth. You fall through
the air until things are right, you answer.
Do you understand life better when you
are high, I ask. You understand that the
whole mystery sucks. Aren't you afraid
of the danger, I ask. My drugs are very
dear to me. Everything sorts itself out
when you're high, you answer. Do you
feel lucky so far not to have died, I ask.
My life resembles a grave. I'm happy to
take the chance, you answer. Are you
ever afraid during a high, I ask. I'm safe.
I know what I'm doing, you answer. How
did your addiction begin, I ask. At fourteen,
my parents introduced me to heroin. My
father died of an overdose, you answer.
May I ask one last question. What is the
likelihood that you will ever seek help,
I ask. Never. I never want to see my life
up close again. And with that answer you
wrap a rubber tube around your forearm,
slip the tip of a silver needle into the basilica
vein.

Drugs and Love

I now understand enough about this love
to shove it away. Once shoulder deep
in romance, I thought I saw rockets when
you walked into a room. Was God pulling
my leg when he pointed me towards you
to fill my empty heart with illusion? Never
once did the contraption we called our
relationship run right. Even though
it had four flat tires at all times, we tried
to drive it anyway. We might have made it
crossing flatland, but we faced mountainous
differences. It took a strong stomach
to swallow the truth about your addiction,
but I made myself stare at needle holes
in your arm that looked like teeth marks
from a poisonous snake. You couldn't
stay clean, and your commitment withered.
I found you walking in the rain toward a
lethal dose and a drug dealer you already
owed money to, put you in the car and
took you to McDonald's before you had
crossed the line. Sitting in the restaurant,
I asked you to describe the sensation you get
from heroin. You said your worries disappear

and you feel warm all over. My patience
stretched tight, and I wanted to throw dollars
on the table and leave. We began haggling
about love, and for the first time I admitted
that it was not enough to compete with your
addiction. I drove you home, studied your
profile when we parked. I have no memory
of saying goodbye. I simply accelerated
and spun rain from wheels until I went
far away from loving you.

You lie against the bricks of a Speedway
station only because the manager is
indisposed and doesn't see your desperation
spread out on the concrete like a ragged
scarecrow. Young though you are, your
face has aged into a sharp poignancy, skin
wrinkled toward heaven as you look up
at the night. Hands under your thighs for
warmth, cold truth of dereliction stays in
your fingers. You begin to grow drowsy,
but the once velvet sleep you took for
granted no longer flowers into peaceful
dreams. Late-night customers pass you
without sympathy. You stare at pants legs,
shoes that ignore you as if you were debris
put out for the Thursday pickup. Days ago,
your heroin-addled girlfriend shut you out
of a shared house, moved in with her
grandma while you packed nothing and
pointed vagrancy toward the street. Rain
puddles on steamy August pavement. You
feel a toe poke through the hole in you sock,
a small feeling of escape from the world
that tossed you to its bottom. Someone

throws you a dollar. It floats to your side
like a broken wing. Flashes of occasional
headlights flame your face like the slap of
someone better off. A sliver of despair
ripples down your empty stomach. What
heart would let you lie here embracing
cement? Could it be the result of people
turning away from your lies and deception,
leaving you to the justice of the streets?
Hope withers like weeds along the curb,
drops of neon stick to stems, your cry
for help hushed as a funeral.

Distraught Desire

I cherish Christ-like moments of each day
when I choose to wear thorns of a miserable
love and suffer memory. A self-imposed
punishment, my personal crucification
nails blame to the damaged prayers I offer
fate, the lame limping away from the wreck
of my heart when your dangerous lies steal
my life and warrant that I shut down the
wicked warehouse of words from which I
take sentences to reconcile, sentences to
settle our differences.

I am consistent as a
steady rain in letting you contaminate the truth.

It should be your underweight body dragging
the cross down South End streets and not mine
hanging on the crucifix of a suburban sunset.

Misery from loss is misery even when loss
is counterfeit.

How do I measure the
authenticity of commitment? In your poverty

you scavenge for stale doughnuts at a
twenty-four hour shop on South High Street,
beg for loose change at a Speedway
during wee hours of destitution. Why did
I contend with such ragged routines?
I cross the border into broken neighborhoods
to be with you, always wondering if my obsession
will survive to daylight. Let me put it this way:

I am drunk on the possibility of resurrection
to avoid an ending and the emptiness of leaving.

Visit

I'm standing on grass in front of the jail
on Jackson Pike. I enter the one-floor
building, show my identification, and wait
for visiting hours to begin. Maybe you
have secured you place in heaven for
writing bad checks. I don't know.

Eventually, guards unlock iron doors,
and I walk down a hall to an alcove
where several visitor's stations remind
me that this is not a normal environment.
I wait.

Soon, you shuffle into view from
your quarters and slouch into a chair behind
a glass partition with a perforated silver
disk we can talk through. We say
hello, but I look at you as if I've never
seen you before. Your hair needs cut.
The brown jumpsuit, indeed, marks
you as a criminal. We exchange a little
information about the few people we
have in common. Even though your green
eyes say welcome, conversation lacks

enthusiasm. I stare and remember
your drug use and negligence, want to yell
out the harm you have done, but, instead, I
pretend that I am loved and continue the
small talk.

Second Visit

I wait in line to visit you a second time
in the Franklin County Correctional
Facility. I have given myself over to
the rules of incarceration and emptied
my pockets into a gray plastic tray. I
feel misplaced as if I've strayed into a
different reality. Nine other people have
lined up behind me.

At noon a locked door clicks open, and
we trudge down a corridor. I settle
at a visiting station and wait for a guard
to bring you down. You appear from
around a corner, slump your lean body
into a chair. The guard stands against
a brick wall, monitoring. A glass panel
between us makes it impossible to embrace,
so we exchange smiles. It occurs to me
to ask why I am here, since the tumultuous
waters of our relationship have mostly
ebbed and flowed, ebbed and flowed.
We take long looks at each other.
There is silence.

My mind drifts, and I think before I leave
I want you to make an incision in my heart,
fill it with whatever little love you ever had
for me.

You bring me back to the moment and
ask me to leave money in you account. I
do not have the power to say no. I rise to
leave, wishing I could cut the slender
thread of longing that still holds me to you.

Incarcerated Angel

Your arms are to your sides as you sit
on a bed slab. Sun through bars stripes
the floor. A roach the size of a candy bar
anchors a brown shadow in the corner.

Your crimes are felonies
of the heart from duplicitous arms
you wrap around unsuspecting victims.
You smile through green eyes
at wrinkled lives that hope to slide a dollar
beneath you waist band after you cool
down from a sweaty dance. Your crimes
are not just theft and forgery but deliberate
murder of the lonely.

What god of seduction sent you to the bar
that night to bare your ripped chest, to rape
the air with the lure of instant love?

You lie on your bunk, stare at the ceiling,
wish you had a cigarette to make clouds
reminiscent of heaven. How humble
your hand, empty now of possibility,
your arm flung out from a bunk like

someone who has sacrificed himself
to defeat. You manipulated lust, made
small talk among the bar crowd like a true
messenger of immoral worship
and human misfortune.

Handling Truth

How many people do you know
who haven't been in prison? I ask.
Some uncles and an aunt, you answer.
The irony is that I am robbing you
of secrets to show you what you already
know, that everyone in your world is
an ex-con. You have not tried to change
environments so much as lament the one
you're in. It rains drugs in your neighborhood,
and sun never brightens faces of those
who need a fix.

We're sitting in Taco Bell, and you show me
the abscess on your arm from a needle.
Nothing needs to be said. I simply stare
and wither, not because your suffering is
unacceptable, but because I do not comprehend
pissing away your life on heroin. A layer of
thick cheese slips from a slice of your Mexican pizza
back into the cardboard box. Your abscess looks
ready to burst with infection, and flies would pester it,
if it were summer. Actually, at that moment,
I want to run away from you and your bad habit,
but I take a deep breath and swallow irritation,

rancor I feel because you've shown me a hint
of death.

We finish eating, and you walk outside
for a smoke. I follow because you asked me to
and because I would feel betrayed by a cigarette
if left inside by myself. So we stand outside
shoulder to shoulder while you puff away
good health, and I refrain from commenting
on habits I do not understand.

Wrong Obsession

Why do you get drunk in front of me?
I love you so much, enough for bliss,
but you drink shot after shot until the bottle
is empty and you are amber-eyed and disoriented.
What secret conflict has you wanting to
escape? What secret love crawls in your
veins to trouble your mind? I wait on
the sidelines, watch you tip the bottle
into glass after glass. When the bottle
is finished, you seek balance, flounder
a bit, find a stationary concentration
and some far away image I can't see.
I never know what you are looking at.
Is it infidelity that makes you see through
a cracked kaleidoscope? Whatever image
you focus on leaves me behind under
the kitchen's fluorescent truth of abandonment.
I wonder how much love it will take to bring
you back, and I worry that I do not have enough
to give because you have siphoned off huge
amounts of my patience and tolerance for pill
and drug addictions. You go to jail under a warrant
arrest. I check inmate information
each day to see if your punishment satisfies

my damaged heart. Now I am tipsy on the toxic
broth of memory, sip each incident, allow
longing into my brain and the desire to be
with you again no matter how dangerous the price.

Lesson

You taught me how to roll a joint.
I sat at the kitchen table watching
you fill the paper, lick it shut.
Crumbs of cannabis disappeared
into the table's wooden cracks when
you swept stray bits into a pile.

You would say, "Ready," and I would
follow you out the back door to the dark
patio. Sometimes you had a lighter.
Other times you asked for stove matches
which you struck in a mortar joint,
leaving a black scar on the house.

Since marijuana was not yet legal in Ohio,
it felt daring and romantic to defy the law.
You believed pot innocuous,
had been doing it since you were twelve.
On the other hand, I had only intermittent
curiosity, a desire to unite us.

Afterwards, you would ask if I wanted
to go into the bedroom, indulged me only
because you knew the drug made me horny.

We dropped our clothes on the floor,
reached for each other's shadows
in semi-dark lit from the hallway.
We never lay together long, but roll away
always with something tender unsaid.

As Does Love

On this late September morning, I wish
I knew why letting you back into my life
makes me feel hollow. I want to know why
I'm not at rest with what is left of our
relationship. Last night, we sat in my car,
and rain fell like coins on the roof. Beneath
clatter of cozy comfort, you lamented how
all of the wrongs of your life result from bad
background. Parents offered you pills at
fourteen, shared heroin at age twenty-four.
I wanted to hold you against my chest and
have your past melt away like perfect magic.
I touched you on the nape of the neck and,
for a few seconds, everything seemed okay.
Leaves blew out of the black night against
the windshield. You got out of the car and
crossed the street, walking a little lopsided
toward the house with cardboard in the
windows and plywood on the door. This is
where you sleep on the floor when you can
afford minimal rent. I drove away
not wanting to leave you to perpetual poverty
and a possible relapse with drugs.

This morning I'm looking out the dining room
window and notice red tinge on plumage
of the dogwood tree, the beginning of death
that burnishes leaves and becomes beautiful.
I keep watching the tree, staring at a thousand
reasons why, in spite of flawed love, there is
no release from you.

The Myth of Intimacy

During winter when trees retained snow
turned to ice, you lay in my bed,
and I lay behind you, my arm across your
chest, your hand over mine. Both of us
fully clothed, we held that position until
we slept.

Throughout the night, ice melted,
and by morning, sun monopolized the room.
I moved, and you awakened. Outside,
trees dripped like ruined sculptures.
At that moment I felt the power of love
in our bodies, but you rose, got a soda
from the refrigerator, went into the living
room, and turned on the television. Your
silence told more than words could have.
I looked at you on the sofa, the soda
on the coffee table. Why wouldn't you
want to be amorous at the opportune time?

You wrestled into your coat, and I drove
you home. We parked at your house, argued
who should have made the first move. Anger
surged like a flash flood. You sprang from the car
and slammed the door.

I recognized the inevitable had begun,
falling away from each other like opposing magnets.
Who to blame for inertia, for not being willing
to connect? At home I looked at the barely
mussed bed and thought of Andrew Marvell's
"To His Coy Mistress."

Indifference and Lies

I am looking at what has ruined me.
In the ash heaps of desire where I
spent many midnights, I found you
lonely as I. You struck a match, lit
a cigarette, and I saw your thin face
illuminated by the burning tip. You
leaned your head through darkness
and against my chest, your breath speaking
small words. The cigarette dangled
from your left hand like a fiery piece
of chalk. You rubbed out the orange
glow against the brick wall, scarring
it with a black smudge. Your half-closed
eyes focused on nothing but saw me
looking at the velvety field of stars
above us. You took a few steps into
the dewy grass, and I followed. You
studied the sky as if just discovering it,
and I raised one of your hands against
my lips inhaling the harsh smell of
nicotine. Your face wore a mask of
stoic deception that I did not recognize
until years later, but on this particular
night I assumed your non-expression

to be the look of peace and not the look
of someone who would never know how
to love.

We entered the shadowy house, and I
turned on a lamp. You asked me to
drive you home, and I did, dumbfounded
that you slept with your head against the
side window, forced to keep affection to
myself.

Have you nothing to say? I don't believe
the dangling cigarette interferes with thought
or speech. For the last two hours you've
looked at every item in the tool department
of Lowe's, and I have followed behind you
waiting for a word scrap, gesture, look.
For want of something to do, I study you
from steps away. The cigarette now behind
your ear gives you the look of a South-End thug.
Crow's feet, shadows under the eyes, lines
around your mouth leave no doubt about
the effects of heroin, a thief that has begun
to steal you're youthful look. Your compelled
to pull your pants up now and then on
emaciated hips. Once a dancer, your body
retains its lithe flexibility as you squat to
examine a tool set. I want to keep my eye
on you. There's something I want to know
that I feel I'll learn from staring. Maybe
I'm waiting to hear you say that you want
to fit into the world of normal people, or
maybe I'm waiting to hear you say why
I am so often invisible to you. You amble
to another aisle, pick up a hand drill and test

its bit in a block of wood. For the fifth time
the clerk asks if he can help. He's bored
but suspicious of the time we've spent
browsing. Nothing purchased, we head
toward the exit, cigarette already sticking
from your lips like a New Year's Eve party
horn. You light up, and I walk away toward
the car, distance myself from your refusal
to take notice.

Showdown

I expected an evening drunk with love,
but you never touched me with eyes, hands,
or thought. It would have been better if you
had asked me for money and left instead of
keeping me at a distance like a trap door you
were afraid you'd fall through if you reached
into my space. I'm living in a second-rate cartoon
wherein I keep getting bounced on my head.

I know you do not want to discuss my pain
which keeps coming back, slapping my heart
each single moment to remind me that I have
learned nothing from unhappiness. You
descend on me like a giant bird and peck dollars
from my pocket. It's pretty much the same
routine every time we meet. I come into your
presence wishing

to show you deepest caring, but you
relegate me to the most incidental afterthought.
You have always been the deepest part of my day,
but you invite nothing from me as tremendous
as a kiss or a hug to assuage my doubt. I will
not argue you into loving me. My blood burns

from wanting you, but I force myself to be stoic.
The night has been anything but good. At the
end of the evening, my eyes bulge with tears.
At the end of the evening, I have
never been so sad.

Wrongness of Revenge

I know to back away from a grudge,
but deep down I want to connect
a metaphorical fist to the person's face
who harmed me. It is you, the heroin addict,
who makes me want to interrupt my life
with anger.

I drove you down dark alleys, waited
in risky neighborhoods while you transected
deals with drug peddlers. You instructed
what to do if police cruised by. It didn't bother
you that I might have ended up in jail,
a naive accomplice. I had become a citizen
of secrecy, someone who loved you enough
to deny the truth of drug-addled lies.
Far away in my mind I knew it was all wrong,
but I wanted to see you again and again, so
I locked myself in the cycle of your addiction.

One spring afternoon I waited in the car
outside Saint Leo's church for you to return
from a side street and someone who promised
you a fix. The church bell rang, and I wondered
had the time come for me to turn it all over to God.

A few days later your front door was unlocked.
I walked in and found you in bed with someone else.

It's a character flaw to think this way, but
I lived in hell for you, sliced my wrist with loneliness.
Now I want revenge, and this poem, if published,
might just be that.

February Evidence

You slipped out of your clothes so easily
with her. Each piece dropped to the floor like
personal insults to the commitment you had
made to me. She videoed your heads coming
together in a practiced kiss. Nothing was
hidden in the shadows or from this infidelity
discovered on your cell phone. I threw the
phone on the bed beside your sleeping
nakedness, furiously shouted for you to dress
and get into the car. Without a license, I had
to drive you home. Your shocked face remembered

I had once shown you a gun in the nightstand.
You screamed justification for your unfaithfulness
and grabbed the gun, pointing it at your head.
My hand locked on yours in a dance with near
death. Slowly, my grip floated your arm downward,
and you released the gun into my fingers.
We sat down facing each other, and you kept
an eye on the gun. Though I listened to your
excuses, you suspected that I was only trying
to slow-talk you away from the gun, out of
the house, and into the car.

On the way to your house, we defaulted to
silence. I pulled up to the curb, turned my
expressionless face toward you and simply
stared. You insisted on offering me another
apology. I said get out.

I drove away from the planet that night unable
to forestall the chill that started in my brain and
dropped to the bottom of my body. It began to
rain, and I snapped on the wipers that couldn't
move fast enough to wipe away downpour
and betrayal.

Severed Hope

I'm crouched in the corner of defeat, swollen
scars of attempting to love you. I
believed in possibilities that would rescue you
from marriage to the muck and mire of streetlife,
from criminal courtship with drug dealers.
You slinked through shadowy alleys after
midnight for the euphoria of a fix, slipped along
tree-lined streets like an addicted phantom to the
door of your next heroin hit. To satisfy me, you
mimicked a sober side, but I walked into your
ramshackle house of blanketed doorways and
boarded windows to find infidelity tucked
under your bed covers and a glass tray of used
syringes.

For days, I let go of your duplicity and deception,
turned away from the lean embrace of your
lying arms, but you held onto my heart with
both hands and pulled me back into the quicksand
of your possession. I became lost in my incapacity
to change you, floundered from one of your secrets
to the next until I found the video on your cell phone
of you making love to someone else. That's when
I banished you from the instant contact of texting

and sobered from my addiction to you. It is not easy to tell myself that once upon a time there was a story in which two people took commitment for granted, drifted apart, and ultimately did not outlast the spring.

Now

I spend ten months looking out a window
as far as I can, trying to forget grief
you cause, trying to prioritize you
out of my life. I almost succeed
in closing the book in which you are
the antagonist, the character who is bad
news until the last sentence. Your unexpected
text catches me off guard, and I can't
concentrate until I answer it. Your woes
haven't changed, and the next thing I know
I open your cage of troubles and cram
dollars into your pocket to pay rent and
afford something to eat. Having the
propensity to rescue someone, to save the indigent,
it is easy to give you the millionth chance.
Of course I reprimand myself and wonder
what the next move will be. Since you are
not a homeless person from the street but
someone with whom I have had a romance,
attraction persists. I begin again to think
of nothing but you. The obsession yells
in my head as if it has a tongue of its own.
Because I meet you for dinner several times,
in a roundabout way, we are heading back

to what I have tried so hard to be free of, the
troubled relationship I thought I'd never escape.

Now it's the end of the month. Tomorrow is
October first, and though I do not want to
fall prey to bad autumn memories, I agree
to pick you up among shabby, rundown, South End
houses, and let my eyes fill and overflow
with your presence. In every direction there are
warnings to let go, but my heart ignores the prod
of fate, and I drop my hand into yours
without any promise of happiness.

The Art of Supplication

I can't imagine sitting across from you
again at Tee Jaye's. You would order biscuits
and gravy with French toast. You would
pull your lips away from hot chocolate
because it was still steaming.

You would keep your
eyes down, looking at indifference, unwilling
to acknowledge that you had loosened me
from sleep at two in the morning. Your
sticky fingers pulled back the metal latch
and you flooded toast with maple syrup
the way you flooded me out of bed with
an appeal to your persistent poverty.

The waitress would float to the table, clad
in obsequious patience, and we would
reassure her that we were doing fine while
all along you were plotting your next deceit.
Eventually I buried my hand in a pocket,
scrambled out a wad of bills, all the cash
I had, and handed it to you like a sacrifice
of good judgment.

I always wanted you
to have something to tide you over until
the next round, and there would be a next
round because of perpetual joblessness.
Like an abused wife I cowered in the
shadow of possibility that you would
someday break free of drug addiction and
background that fed you pills from age twelve.

No. I will never meet you again, and your
phone calls will go unanswered while you
suffocate alone with your false pleas for a
better life.

Perilous Rendezvous

Dan's Drive-In is boarded-up, but you asked me
to meet you there. I do not know why I agreed.
To keep you from suicide? To learn how little or
much I cared? I'm parked facing the direction
from which you will walk. Behind me plywood
windows are stark, still like dead eyes.
When you finally come into view wearing a
sleeveless t-shirt, tattoos, hair in need of a trim,
you wait for heavy traffic to pass before you can
cross the street.

In the car your profile is still the same young look,
the same innocence that caused me to deny your
drug addiction. It's been ten months since the death
of our relationship, and I shelved any possibility of
reconciliation like a bad novel I disguarded.
We drive around the South End for awhile,
talk about your job and your deficits. I want to hold
you as I would a child and cradle you from abuse
that has been your life so far.

We stop at Great Clips for your haircut, eat at
Ponderosa, pay your overdue phone bill. Then,
I hand you a little pocket cash and hope that it

won't be used for heroin. What purpose did I
serve in picking you up? Preventing suicide?
Enabling worst habits? Supporting you on the
path to rehabilitation?

You hug me before getting out of the car. I'm
frozen in place with sadness. I drive home and
the same sadness sits on the seat beside me like
a real person. It follows me into the house, watches
me get ready for bed, sidles up beside me in the
darkened dining room, and we watch out the window
as if waiting for a conclusion.

Gravity

I want to abracadabra myself away
from the lure of you. Instead, the mind chants
words that obligate my heart? Those words
are an interior life I live as I go about
folding laundry and scrubbing floors.
I do not like being caught up in an obsession.
Between arguments we have few beautiful
moments, and silence clings like a poisonous
vine to most of our conversations. Each
of my attempts to leave you boomeranged,
and I returned knowing that loving you
was the only thing I knew how to do.
Even sex felt like an obligation. So why
haven't I let you go? Why do I quiver
inside when I see you? It can only mean
one thing when I boil down the reasons.
No one but you jolts my blood with the ache
of longing. You have always drawn me toward
your magnetic center as if I were a pin or
paperclip. It seems futile denying feelings
that keep surfacing, so I will let you pull me
to your side again and finally this time half
believe it is where I belong.

Lassitude

A blade of sun slices through the window,
carpets hardwood floor in yellow light.
Even though everything outside is wind-blown,
late October leaves have not yet twisted down
from trees.

I'm sitting in a chair facing the sun.
It is one of those days when my life feels
as if it's at a standstill. I step back from
any direction I consider turning in, too
dejected to write a poem, too despondent
to go outside.

I believe failure to have a
successful relationship with a heroin addict
is why I'm looking at myself with downcast
eyes. Because of imperfect love
I tumbled into hell, a place where needles
mean as much as breath.

I sit here at the window
and say these things. I want to say more
to free myself of rage and resentment
for how you tainted me with street life.

I used every word in the dictionary
to pry you away from addiction. It would
have been easier to pull a nail from a board
with my teeth. Along the way I learned
that I cannot help you become clean.

What's left of the day might yet be saved if I stop
this commentary and silent hurt. Wind is
still shaking clouds loose, moving them along
at an even pace. Tree shadows are lengthening
across the lawn, marking time like a sundial.
Tonight the moon will be as full and round
as a baby's face, and maybe by then I will have
arrived at somewhere better.

Rough

Drab, bent over lives on straight back chairs await
their turn at the drug rehab clinic. Like candle wax,
faces have melted into masks of despair. Most
manipulate cell phones, twitch legs, shake feet.
It's a rare person without multiple tattoos that sneak
from short sleeves and out of cuffs like initiation rights
into a special club.

A name is called and someone disappears through
a door for a drop. Much of three hours is spent
with elbows on knees and head in hands waiting.
An overweight woman with thighs big as wastebaskets
waddles through the front door with a plastic grocery bag
on her arm. She's taken a break from opiates to sell candybars
for her middleschool nephew. None of the stoic heads turn
to buy, and she settles into ubiquitous wait.

It is an oppressed room enslaved by habit.
Gumball and m&m machines positioned against
a gloomy green wall lure no one, their innocuous
multicolor fix ignored. If patients were to chant, would they
chant a mantra for answers, for a perminant solution
to substance dependancy, or would they prefer
to keep silent and let cold chill sit upon their skin.

Wounded Roses

There are days when you make me hate
even the sun. I give you roses, and you
shred them in front of me. Petals tremble,
land at my feet, mocking. This is how
it always is, a ruinous inclination in you.

Promises die in your mouth.
I'm afraid there is more suffering in store,
if I don't quit seeing you again and again.

Maybe if I walk a street in a neighborhood
I've never been in, I'll stop remembering.
My obsession with you is like an additional organ,
an arm, a leg. It is something that is simply there
like rain or regret.

Street-Weary Intrusion

All day my mind floods with thoughts of you.
From the time I got up this morning, I've let you
stalk my heart. I'm overcome by your absence.
Friends would condemn me for sparing one minute
to consider what could have been with you.
I'm choking on crazy words, ones that put aside
resentment and still want an ex-con burnt out
on drugs. Once I scrubbed you from my life
like a bad stain, I swore I would stay clean
of your corruption.

You took me down a labyrinth of alleys,
made me wait in shadowy neighborhoods
full of boarded-up houses decayed like
a mouthful of rotten teeth, gave me nothing
but failed love and hurt from infidelity.

I am weak with obsession, search
for you in every corner of memory.
It is extremely wrong to want to see you.
You are a thief who wrote bad checks,
stole five years of my life, but I am fragile
as an autumn fly, ashamed of vulnerability,
of wanting to share the same space with you again.
It's always been a rule to let the dead alone.
I buried you once. Today I exhumed you
and suffocate.

Obsession Is a Slow and Constant Song

The house is silent, but a field of locusts whir
in my head. Tinnitus once took me to a psychiatrist
who gave me medicine to stop inner noise.
Tonight, however, locusts drone particularly loud
because my stress level is off the chart.

A hundred times today you occupied my thoughts.
I would sooner fall down a ravine, lie there
undiscovered, then have you in my life.
Yet, I know that's a lie. I would rather take a gun
and shoot the hell out of sunlight then not
ever see you again.

You packed lies into every sentence,
ripped up trust as if it were an unwanted
handbill. I linger in horror, unable to handle
that you had sex with a heroin-addicted blonde.

The real truth is I want you,
but I don't want you in my life. That
contradiction can only be understood
by anyone who's ever been happy
to be unhappy.

For months I have lived free of you, but
I forget none of the misery you caused.

It is my mood tonight that wants you back,
a temporary relapse that works against
the very possibility.

The Epitome of Loss

I see outside what I've become, a dreary
November day. I am wordless and clogged
with emotion. I want to become unobsessed
with you, vanish slow pain that seeps through
me like blood. The loss of you is electrical
throughout my entire body. Why is it difficult
to let go of something that did not work
in the first place. I cannot kill blues that sings
through me like a dirge. I cannot stay focused
on anything but you. Distractions have little value.
Longing is a constant unmanageable ache.

I look outside at squirrels. They cavort, bury acorns,
know how to love without loving. There is no wind.
Leaves are dead on the ground. The possibility of
never seeing you again opens a fissure in my heart
I fall into second after second.

Dangerous Moonlight

Moon broken by winter oak branches patterns
our faces with ashen light, luminescence
bright enough to walk through a cemetery.
We are a mile from there, standing on
my driveway. A spidery feeling crawls
within my gut because I have no prayers
to save us.

Yesterday I sat on a bench in that cemetery
watching a mother and her kid place flowers
at the foot of a black tombstone, felt we, too, had
handed our relationship over to a gravedigger.

You take a drag from a cigarette, and I remark
how much I hate that you smoke. We are moody
as the dead trying to come alive, our zombie hearts
zagged by defeat. You inhale, flick an ash.

We once believed compatibility possible,
until you slept with someone else.
I backed away from your smooth lies, admitted
a trailing off of love.

Our eyes don't meet. Moonlight continues
to drench us. A train whistle repeats
in the distance, a sound as sorrowful as a whippoorwill,
a train that I wish would carry me out of this sad place.

When Nothing Is Left but Addiction

What do I find inside my heart if I bisect it?
I find love for you kidnapped by infidelity.
All that remains is a shell of blood,
footprints leading to someone else. I died for you.
shrank down to a gaunt facsimile of myself,
having sacrificed even food to give you money.
I want to make a mantra of these words:
Let it go. Let it go.

I can smell the drifting smoke of your cigarette
in the black night and stiffen with chill. My
whole body reacts to loss, ripples a burning cold
because I can't accept that you are sleeping with
someone else.

I'll sum it up this way: I still find you
in every corner of my mind. Your face never
blurs. It follows me all day.

One morning I hope to awaken without you
in my thoughts. I want to heal, so when I hear
your name, no darkness comes over me.
I want to obliterate obsession and stop
coming back to the belief that we could
have grown beyond our differences.

Bricks, Sticks, Stones

I built a wall around emotions,
bricks, sticks, stones. It crumbles
whenever I think of you. No
mental tool lifts me away from
speculation. Where are you? What
are you doing? With whom? I call
it obsession equal to addiction.

I survived a gangster's love
or machinations that passed for love.
I want a deeper solution whereby
even my release from memories of you
becomes permanent and complete like
finality when dirt is backhoed into a grave.
I want to find no scraps of you in my skull.

These thoughts unbutton me from sleep,
remain through breakfast and the rest of
the day. How could God have made a
world with you in it, brain darkened by
drugs, decades of deception and lies,
a moth-like instinct that attracts you
not to light but to someone's money?
They call your type a gigolo or user.

You had no magic, just the lure of youth
that shimmered on you like an invitation
to trust. I chose to trust.

Now I choose a different truth that leaves
a wrecked relationship a dwindling mirage in
the desert of forgetfulness. In a matter of time
I will search through ruins you left behind
for definite proof of your absence,
for disfigured fragments of my heart.

Consuming Passion

They used to stack stones to mark a grave.
The death of our relationship is identifiable
by boulders, stacks and stacks of boulders.
I promise myself each hour not to think
about you, to take deep breaths and entomb
the past. I wear flush of frustration, feel
chill of loss in my gut. This is when I wish
my imagination were dead too because I
can picture you learning to love someone
else.

There are a million reasons why
we did not fit together. There are a million
reasons that define the downfall of us,
yet I would push away common sense for
another start.

Some days I become non-functional, lying
about the house, trying magically to know
if you ever think of me. Even someone of
God's powers can't hand you to me
if you don't want to be there.

So I will burn with desire as if tired to a stake
of longing, and you will inhale the smoke and
know that my sacrifice was complete, that I gave
everything I had, and still I could not hear your voice
because you did not speak.

Blame

I do not think I stumbled past love
without knowing it. I understand now
I would have been better off with
someone else. That's how love works.
I went in a straight line to the wrong person.
I rolled up sleeves, gave your indifference
a good try.

You did a myriad things to defeat me:
lied, always withheld truth. It doesn't
matter any more that you took everything
from me except blood. I stopped telling
you not to devour your body with drugs.
I left without a proper goodbye.

Because of out extreme age difference,
I will never know when you pass. I will,
most likely, go first. Deception was our
foe and finally infidelity.

I have a long journey before I cross the bridge
of forgetfulness. Each day your name sings
in my head like a poisoned song that kills
and kills and kills. I want out of the cage

I've put myself in. I want to defy memory,
plant it in the ground and let weeds smother it.
Without you I'm neither dead nor alive, just old
and embarrassed by regret.

The addicted ones we've loved have twisted us.
I sit around a table with twelve others
at an Al-Anon meeting. We are at the bottom
of stillness waiting for the first person to speak.
This is our home when we are here. The chaos
of failure has written a calm defeat on our faces
because we have come to recognize and accept
that not a sliver of caring makes the addict
clean. There is no neutrality in the world
of drugs. No matter how deep under skin
we burrow, blood keeps addressing addiction.

It is the user's bent to cover up the sun
with a black cloth, to keep shadowy secrets
to himself. It is imperative to lovingly ignore
the wounded, stand aside and take for granted
the requisite commitment required to rescue
himself from false dreams of a drug's
golden hours. We at the table have learned
patience, have told our stories, tucked in
defeat, and await the time when sobriety will be
resurrected. We have experienced the harshest
outcomes, been torn to shreds by the mad effort
to make a difference. We have chosen out of
despair to be together at this table and in our
humblest way welcome the pageantry of hope.

At the Al-Anon Meeting

They smile at me, tiny smiles,
but smiles. Truth is going to sail
around the room like a crippled ship,
afloat but hesitant. Whose secrets
should I tell first, mine or the addict's?
Blinds are pulled. It wouldn't matter
because it's 7:15 on a November evening,
and night, like a seducer, has stripped light
from day.

It seems years go by before I speak.
Mouth dry, words stick in my throat.
"I'm in a harmful relationship with a heroin
addict who has poisoned my heart."
The room is quiet as if everyone has stopped
breathing, the moment more than confession.
I continue to speak to faces tender
with acceptance. I still have much to say.
It will take many sessions, but I have
put a little piece of anguish behind me.

We end holding hands with people
on either side of us, recite"The Lord's Prayer."

Afterwards, hugs exchanged, an overwhelming
sense of camaraderie pervades the room.

I trudge to my car and drive home. Alone in my house
I remember what I have said, feel a little less
devoured by an all-consuming love.

Dream Song

My speech to God is about resentment.
In spite of Al-Anon, I dream angry dreams.
In one you were dressed in a suit and tie,
standing beside an older man also dressed
in a suit. You who only knew South End
gangster attire dawdled on the curb across
from me. I'd just finished talking to the
proprietor of the bar where the front window
had been completely broken out by delinquents
the night before. I had stopped to inquire
of her if she knew your whereabouts, and
there you were, your stoic face impervious
to wrongdoing, to wounds you slashed my
my psyche with. We didn't speak. I stared
at your cruelty, lies, deception, infidelity,
and then walked on down the street out
of sight.

I awoke distorted as if from one of your drugs
and wanted the satisfaction of retaliation
if for no other reason then you had interrupted
my sleep with you hands-down pose of indifference.
All day I saw you, not dream-like, dragging me
by the heart down the same street, but that was
a dream, too, wasn't it. That was a dream.

Workman

A workman will soon arrive to fix
the water pump in the basement. He won't
suspect that I feel as if I've fallen
onto the moon and hit the bottom of
a crater, or that I've been plowed under
by a farm tractor that didn't see me.
The question is why I would despair
over a toxic relationship that was best ended.

I have not learned yet to let go of the edge
of glass.

Bloody fingers seem incidental
to retaining the only long-term partner
I've ever had. There are eight bottles of beer
in the refrigerator. That may be enough
for a bit of oblivion but not enough for me
to let go of unlucky love. If I could kill

passion and desire, the need for you would
vanish. I could stand at the window,
look out at today's pounding rain, and not feel
lost. My life has no pivotal point
without you. It is early April, but tree limbs
are still bare.

The workman is finished and trudges up
basement steps, edges of his boots crusted
with old mud. He is lucky to have something
mechanical to occupy his mind. I pay him,
and he leaves. Did he see the curious look
of pain sweep across my eyes before he left?
Did he suspect the suicidal direction in which
my demons are leading me?

Snow Will Come to Heal

Winter has taken all the leaves away,
and only bare trees witness the dying.
Breathing against the frosted window,
I watch velvet snow fall. Crackle of
logs in the stone fireplace interrupt
silence. I long to embrace the cold,
bring it to my skin and hold it there
until it becomes as warm as a lover.
Sometimes I create my own cold
when I turn away from the mistake
of you that has turned into an obsession.
Fingers of frost fringe the window, a
canvas on which to draw a heart that
is easily erased because I have had enough
of your negligence and its chill of mistrust.
I've grown a new heart and buried the old
one in earth as hard as the effort to eliminate
the hold you've had over me. I have
triumphed over the spell, squeezed you
out of everything I remember, thickened
my defenses against the reblooming of
a love worn away by faithlessness.

Snow rolls past the window, flakes big
as mock orange blossoms. I watch them
accumulate like memories that pile up
in the brain. They mean more than they
should. I will dream of someone new
who will hold my hand in winter's white
places, who will kiss you away along with
all the other unbeautiful lies of my life.

Outcome

Your parents placed them on your tongue,
amphetamines at fourteen, creating
the beginning of a lifelong addiction.
They watched you poke fire into your veins,
handed you the needles. You could not escape
the smoke of their cigarettes, and so lit your own
at age nine. Thereafter, you carried yourself like
a South End hood, sleeveless t-shirt, tattoos, and
low-slung pants. Whether on ice or in rain,
your innards cried out for a fix, and you walked
alleys and streets to find dealers. No wonder
you came off as a loser, your face locked into
a belligerent mask that challenged the world.
You stared at the river, wondering if you could
end it there. The rubble of your life somehow
stopped you. However discouraged, you
handed yourself over to minimal hope,
but rehab everyday didn't help you and you relapsed
over and over and over.

Glass Fingers

We exist together under the same sky,
but to you, stars are only so many cigarette burns.
It's beautiful to look at the sky, but tonight, clouds
come apart like heartbreak. I've seen enough
death to know where we're headed. Watching
the sky is not reconciliation. This is a black night
free of pretense when moonlight freezes us into truth.
Clouds have eaten my heart, and there is nothing
left but the burn holes of stars blinking, blinking.
The moon gave us anger and love, and I
will love you until the world fills with water,
and then I will hate God. I am touching the end
of us with glass fingers, the most delicate touch
you will ever feel. Don't forget it, and don't
expect it from someone else. It won't be there.
I'm a single man in a halo of light meant for
lovers. The moon can be so cruel. Ask me,
I know.

Goodbye

You reach for me from the rapture of heroin,
and for the first time in our relationship I
reject you. I do not lie back content with
myself for standing ground. Instead, I listen
to the gears of my mind grind out regret
because love alone will not save you
from the needle. If arms could talk, yours
would cry tears from the hundreds of holes
you've punctured them with.

Today, claws of defeat sink into my heart,
pull it from my chest when you announce
your intention of buying more dope
from your landlady. She pesters you with promises
of euphoria, wants to reel you in as a constant
customer even when you don't have the money.

Tonight you will be high again, and I will hate
the heroin whore for seducing you.
What recourse do I have but to pull back,
let you fall.

I walk away and leave your secrets,
your dealers, drug transactions. No more

will I watch you hand back hours
spent in rehab for another hit.

I have to leave you to futility.

Heaven is not in your arm.

Midnight

I prowled streets until after midnight,
never meant to live this way with hands
in my pocket, looking for another $5.25
for Jack and Coke. When I reached deep,
I found rainwater and crumpled notes
I wrote to you in despairing moments.
Those who know me would think with a few
drinks I've turned into Satan, but I'm not Satan.
I'm a good person who has built a flamboyant
hell for myself' from loving you.

You use heroin needles as bookmarks for the
Bible. I don't sing for you anymore. I sing
for myself, but I still ask around if anyone
has seen you. I ask that question enough
to know you haven't mastered enough sobriety
to stop using.

Last year you lay down with another heroin addict.
Discovering it on Facebook twisted my heart,
poisoned it with finality, and that is why
I scream in my head. Stop! Stop! Stop!

Taco Bell

You drifted into my life again at the end
of autumn. Your pockets were empty
as usual, claimed you hadn't eaten
for days. I knew that wasn't a scheme.
You hadn't worked for a couple of years.

Lies, deception, and infidelity stopped me
from responding to your texts and phone calls.
I got waylaid when you called from a number
I did not recognize and answered it.

I had given you countless chances to patch
our relationship, but you refused to stop using
heroin. Yet here we sat across the table
from one another in Taco Bell. You ordered
a Mexican pizza, ate it as if starved. You knew
it mattered to me if you smoked, still you left
the table, went outside, and let a cigarette.

Was I thinking correctly to wonder where
you got money for cigarettes? Because
I once said I competed with a cigarette
for your attention, you invited me outside with you.

We were standing in the light of the Taco Bell
sign when a pickup truck slowed down, and
my cousin yelled out the window, "Aha. Caught,"
referring to the pledge I'd made never to see you again.

We got into my car, and you pushed back
the seat and slept. Having not been together
for awhile, I resented your shut eyes that dismissed us.
By the time I dropped you off, my heart had
hardened into grudge for being foolish enough
to give you yet another chance.

Looking at Now

I'm giving God the upper hand, mindful
of passivity in doing that. It is October,
and mornings are frosty, afternoons
reminiscent of spring, but I've brought him
into my mind before claustrophobic winter
sets in and forces me to face broken
happiness. I have reached a point where I
feel powerless to terminate an injurious
relationship. I am bewildered about how
to say no to an addict who will soon want
to reenter my life. Because the attraction
is addictive, I cannot bring myself to
throw up the necessary boundries. It is
as if the talons of a formal commitment
have carried off common sense the way
a bird would take its prey into the sky.

I want out of a dark and bottomless hole
I've lived in for more than four years,
a hole where the only illumination came from
a match to light a cigarette. I do not smoke,
so even that cigarette was someone else's
pleasure. As I talk about this, determination
is rising up like a tsunami, and I hope that

when it crashes down, it will wash away
my vulnerability. Why is is so hard to be
negative when my very welfare is on the line?
I'm teaching myself that there is a limit
to romance even when the feelings are
overwhelming, and I'm teaching myself
not to peer into the past but to prepare
for saying what has to be said which is
finally becoming as apparent as lightning.

Strong winds tumble leaves against the windshield.
It is difficult to open the car door against gales
that gust from the West. Weathermen predict
tornado-type activity. You are packed and ready
for your brother to drive you to West Virginia
and away from heroin connections you have
in Ohio. It is your last effort to get clean.

All afternoon we exhaust every resource from
which we can get enough money to pay
for your doctor's appointment at the drug
rehab clinic. Finally, I sign on the dotted line
for a loan from a quick cash place on Parsons
Avenue, a rough part of town.

All the while, you suck on cigarettes, wallow
in withdrawal from Suboxone, recline on the car seat.
Your head thrown back and mouth agape, you resemble
a corpse, someone who has died from an overdose.
This is the way you keep me company, and it
is only one of your thousand abuses.

I mention that your daughter would be upset
if she knew about your drug addiction. You

think that I'm telling you that you never think
of her. Your volatility explodes, you fly
from the car, stand in the street and curse me.
I retaliate with personal insults. You slam
the car door, threatening to kick it in.

I swerve away and charge down the street
like Stoney Roberts, discard our relationship
like a coat worn to shreds. I shovel you out
of my life like dirty snow, profess that I will
never speak of our potential happiness again.

Looking for the Body of What Is Dead

Like rain, love, when it stops, it stops.
Certainly there is no catching up.
Do I wish for a serene burst of reconciliation?
No. Up close, the plot in the book of us is ragged.
I said more goodbyes to you than hellos. Our
relationship has been on rough water for
over four years. You violate your veins
with heroin, hang with people who are blunt
about their addictions and offer you
every opportunity to share their habits, and
you participate rather then be alone. Shortly
after I met you, I became aware of
your addictive habits but not of the magnitude
of your heroin use.

I'm sitting here looking at a pot of plastic
daisies and realize that I feel plastic too,
or maybe a better word is numb because
I have drained all of my feeling into helping
you get clean. This morning I suddenly
knew I would probably never see you
again since you went to West Virginia.
Always our relationship has been a flower
on a broken stem, a loose button threatening

to drop from a coat which it did a few
days ago when you winged my car door shut
and barked obscenities because I tried to
emphasize how you're wasting your life.
That's the night you went to West Virginia,
and I sped away from ever caring
for you again and from the thousand abuses
I mistook for love.

Caring for What Is Lost

I flounder in the weeds of life's garden,
caged in my own emotions. Though you
are with your brother in West Virginia
and away for awhile from bad
people on the street, your voice whispers
to me, and I surrender to the unbearable
possibility that we may never see each
other again. I reached out to you so often
not realizing that I was only enabling
your worst habits. I preached, became you
personal missionary to no avail. Until
you went away, you were a cork bobbing
around in a sea of heroin, surrendering
to the habit, collapsing into yourself
more each day.

The night you left, we parted
like opposing magnets. Anger flamed out of
you as if you were on fire with retribution.
I had asked you if you had ever seen you
addiction through your young daughter's
eyes, and you thought I said that you never
think of her. You ripped yourself from my car,
yelled obscenities and slammed the door shut

on our relationship. I should probably thank
God for any kind of exit from you, since you
had become my addiction. I should have
begged God years ago to release me from you.
Instead, I hid the toxicity of us in the deep
pocket of denial and continued to wait
on streets and in alleys while you negotiated
drugs. Though I will miss the part of my
identity that you have become, these days
I passionately pray for indifference.

Snow

I see first flakes around ten at night.
Their caathedral-like silence whitens
the landscape. In less than an hour,
an accumulation has transformed
even the ugliest structure into
temporary sculpture. Telephone wires
become fluffy tinsel while streets and
sidewalks disappear. According to
forecasts, this is just the beginning of
an eight-inch buildup. Since I lost you
to heroin, you cannot be here
with me to watch the world remake itself
into colorless monotony. I'm learning
to live without your phone calls and texts,
without your touch. You are staying at
your brother's in West Virginia to face
the challenge of getting clean. Ohio was
rife with too many connections. Here,
your fix was inescapable. Because
we tore each other apart with fierce words
before you left, I don't expect to see you
again. Drugs poisoned our relationship,
and it died a slow and miserable death
as if laced with arsenic.

I bundle up to go outside and sweep
the porch steps. Streetlight casts a patina
of glitter across the lawn. I break off a
small branch from the dogwood tree
and use it to write the word pain in the snow,
hoping that when the snow melts, the deepest
hurt I've ever know will disappear.

When Deprived of Someone

Somewhere at the end of a gravel road
is the edge of the earth, and I've fallen off
of it, and I keep falling and falling until I
hit the bottom of bitterness. I crave the
crash because I don't know how to live
in the world without you. My temper
and unhappiness sent you away, and now
I pray to know what I will do on a deep
winter night or on a spring day burning
with blossoms. We were mismatched
in a hundred ways, but now I don't know
how to digest my loneliness. It goes on
and on.

The hours are bones I'm trying to bury.
They are dead with the weight of losing you.
I'm driving my car to get away from what I
don't understand and park on a rural road.
Looking out over Ohio's perfect fields,
November's translucent light, I want to open
the door and run back to where I was once
with you.

Loss is not a beautiful thing. Loss is wanting
to return to the old story and all of its details

and even the pain itself. I am almost peaceful
out here looking at the fields, except that
I imagine reaching for you beside me.
That is when I ask if I am actually preparing
for your return, your blank stare, the very
little love you gave? I open the car door,
step off the berm and into a field of corn
stubble. Everywhere I look there is corn
stubble. The corn is gone and the stocks
are broken.

Ice Town

Except for a myocardial infarction,
which some also believe you caused,
you have brought about all of my hurt
for the last five years. You pounded a nail
in the pulp of my heart with the hammer
of heroin addiction, couched beautiful words
in unconscionable intent to use me.
I was your primary enabler who thought I could
buy you a different life with constant pocket money.

You are nothing more than a South End hood,
a five-times convicted jailbird without conscience.
My admonitions and attempts to help bounced off
you like gymnasts from trampolines.

Twice since I've blocked your phone number and
Facebook page, you've left voicemails asking me
to return your calls. I blush embarrassment at your
audacity to elbow back into my life after all the misery
you triggered.

Any words I have for you reduce to one: No.
You are an unholy source of my sadness, a person with
nothing to offer but detritus of a wasted life. Listen hard.
Whatever I thought was once possible between us is gone,
dissolved like salt in water.

Bus Ride

I ask you to let me know how you are
doing once you settle into a bus seat.
I have wired you money for a ticket. I don't
like to think of you as a drifter, but you
haven't worked for over two years. You
tell me by cell phone that you are sitting
in front of Kroger, cold, wet, hungry, waiting
for money I have sent via Western Union.
You want to travel back to Columbus, Ohio
from your brother's in St. Albans, West Virginia,
a place where you thought you could stay clean.
You claim to have been clean these last weeks.

We spend over six hours texting
in a tug-of-war. You have no one else
to turn to for money. I don't trust you,
so it matters to me how you use the money.
We translate differences into vitriol, harsh
language, icy words, and finally apology.
I don't know your specific destination or
even where you will spend the night.
You have dwelled on the street before,
begged at a Speedway station, know
where to get the drugs you need.

It's getting late, and I haven't heard from you
since you received money. Maybe you
will tell me tomorrow about the trip, whether
your life is worth anything to you anymore.
It rained all day. The bus could be late. I
would settle for a quick text. We used to be close.
Now our connection amounts to a money exchange.
I picture you, head lulling in sleep within
a yellowish aura inside the bus.
Maybe you never boarded the bus.

Days later on Facebook I learned that you spent
the night at the Mardi Gras Casino and Resort in
West Virginia, using my money to celebrate
a one-year anniversary with someone else,
both of you sticking needles into you arms
again and again and again.

Final Thoughts at the End

I surrender to melancholy.
I could understand if it were a matter
of a good thing coming to an end, but
a bad thing coming to an end should
bring joy.

It's morning, and the dark of early winter
falls to pieces when I light a lamp.
Something has broken from the sky, a wren,
I think, and I wonder if its day will be useless too

You are miles away, and though we
are past reconciliation, I nod to
memories that jangle in my mind like
coins in a pocket. Your nicotine-stained
fingers, I called them smoker's hands,
you held out to me palms up to illustrate
poverty, said you hadn't eaten in days,
hornswoggled money from me for
heroin.

I promised myself that I would not write
about you again. So why am I?

Because my failure to lead you to sobriety
holds me prisoner. I will say nothing more.

Where you go in this world will remain
a mystery to me. I do not want to know
what becomes of you. Each day I teach
myself the truth that we are dead, and I am
waiting patiently for us to be buried.

Last Words

The night I dropped you off at Tee Jaye's restaurant
you uttered three syllables with the greatest lack
of meaning I'd ever heard. You could have said
I hate you, and it would have meant as much.

You strode across the rain-slick parking lot,
turned back, threw those words at me again.
I whipped out of the lot, rejected
the greatest lie I'd ever heard.

Nowadays I don't know if you are still
in Columbus or in West Virginia hobnobbing
with other hop heads. Every time I see
someone with a cigarette, I think of
expense and effort I wasted to pull you away
from habit

Cigarettes in the gutter are a reminder
of my failure. I gave you everything
a human being can give another, and
I gave it only to learn later in Al-Anon
what a crippling enabler I'd been.

You are probably somewhere needing food,
shelter, someone whose compassion includes
boundaries. On rainy nights, like tonight,
I still think of you crossing that parking lot
out of my life.

Your broke me in all ways.
I lost faith. Now when I look into God's eyes
I see a stranger.

Going Back

I drift into the bar as if lost,
and in some ways I am. It's been four years
since I've been here. Renovations have
made it a less seedy place to down a Jack
and Coke. There are now colored globes
at intermittent spots on the bar, dim enough
to add a layer of youth to someone facing
them. Two middle-age, very loquacious
men lounge six seats from me to the right.
Otherwise, I'm the only other person there
besides the bartender. Behind the bar is
the proverbial mirror in which I see an
elderly man holding hands with memory.

I turn my head to the left and see a raised
platform where you danced the night we
met. It feels as if I have brought a mental
net in which to catch and drag home bits
and pieces of the past, to prove to myself
that I didn't just imagine the whole toxic
relationship in which I pronounced you
the love of my life.

It is only ten 'o clock,
but there is no sense in hanging around

to see who comes in next because I'm
not here for someone new. I'm here
because the heaviness of being alone
sometimes gets to be too much to bear,
and because I want to see who I am
without you. One Jack and Coke is enough
time to tell me that I am whipping myself
with sadness for no good reason.
It was within these walls that I put our
lives together by mistake.

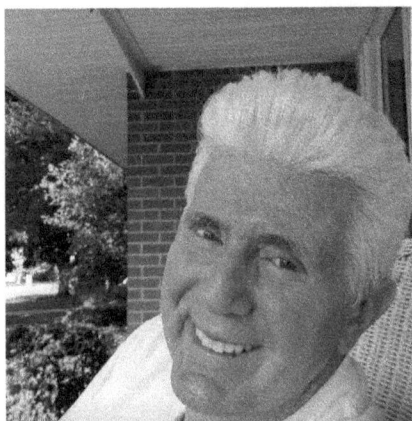

About the Author

R. Nikolas Macioci earned a PhD from The Ohio State University, and for thirty years taught for the Columbus City Schools. In addition to English, he taught Drama and developed a Writers Seminar for select students. OCTELA, the Ohio Council of Teachers of English, named Nik Macioci the best secondary English teacher in the state of Ohio. Nik is the author of two chapbooks: *Cafes of Childhood* and *Greatest Hits,* as well as seven books: *Why Dance, Necessary Windows, Cafes of Childhood* (the original chatbook with additional poems), *Mother Goosed, Occasional Heaven, A Human Saloon, and Rustle Rustle Thump Thump.* Critics and judges called *Cafes of Childhood* a "beautifully harrowing account of child abuse," but not "sentimental" or "self-pitying," an "amazing book," and "a single unified whole." *Cafes of Childhood* was submitted for the Pulitzer Prize in 1992. In addition, more than two hundred of his poems have been published here and abroad in magazines and journals, including *The Society of Classical Poets Journal, Chiron, Concho River Review, The Bombay Review,* and *Blue Unicorn.*

He won First Place in the 1987 National Writer's Union Poetry Competition, judged by Denise Levertov, First Place in The Baudelaire Award Competition, sponsored by The

World Order of Narrative and Formalist Poets (1989), Second Place in Zone 3's first annual Rainmaker Awards, judged by Howard Nemerov (1989), and Second Place in the Writer's Digest annual competition, judged by Diane Wakoski (1991).